I0146271

Augustine W. Wright

In Memoriam

John S. Wright

Augustine W. Wright

In Memoriam
John S. Wright

ISBN/EAN: 9783337120405

Printed in Europe, USA, Canada, Australia, Japan

Cover: Foto ©ninafisch / pixelio.de

More available books at **www.hansebooks.com**

In Memoriam.

OHN S. WRIGHT,

AN ADDRESS

Delivered before the Chicago Historical Society,
Friday Evening, July 21, 1885.

BY

AUGUSTINE W. WRIGHT.

CHICAGO:
FERGUS PRINTING COMPANY.
1885.

CHICAGO HISTORICAL SOCIETY.

CHICAGO, July 23, 1885.

AUGUSTINE W. WRIGHT, Esq.,

Dear Sir:—I have the honor, in behalf of the Chicago Historical Society, to tender to yourself and brother its thanks for the beautiful oil portrait of your father, the late John S. Wright, which you generously presented at the quarterly meeting on the 21st inst.

I also beg to inform you that, on the motion of Hon. William Bross, the thanks of the Society were unanimously tendered to you, and a request made that you furnish a copy of the biographical memoir of your father which you read on that occasion, that the same may be published.   Very respectfully,

ALBERT D. HAGER,
Secretary.

In Memoriam.

JOHN S. WRIGHT.

Gentlemen of the Chicago Historical Society and Ladies and Gentlemen:

I HAVE the honor of addressing you this evening upon the life of my father, the late John S. Wright, although I realize fully the truth of Barham's statement, that "It may, perhaps, be questioned whether under any circumstances a very near relative is a fit person to fill the office of biographer; independently of the prepossession by which he must almost necessarily be swayed, and of the restraint which a consciousness of its existence induces, expressions both of eulogy and the reverse seem to fall ungracefully from his pen. The writer has no immunity to plead in the present instance from the effects of this law."

In 1832, the population of Chicago was estimated at 150. Today it is estimated at 700,000! What has caused this wondrous growth, a growth unequalled in rapidity by any city of the known world? Some will answer, it is due to nature, to the wonderful natural advantages surrounding the site upon which this proud city was to be erected. I, however, affirm that it is to be attributed not less to the remarkable character of those who, in the early days, ventured from their homes into this almost unknown region and by their wonderful energy and unequalled ability gave an impetus to the growth of the would-be city, that has gathered force as it rolled, and has resulted in the Chicago of today!

"The means that heaven yields must be embraced, and not neglected; else if heaven would and we will not, heaven's offer we refuse."

No city was ever the happy possessor of greater capacity in its founders! John S. Wright wrote, "A set of men superior to the early settlers of Chicago were never brought together." Only the most enterprising and energetic ventured upon the long and trying journey to the then "Far-West", and those early settlers have left their impress upon every profession, every occupation in the life of this great metropolis! Their fame is not bounded by the confines of this vast continent, but has extended to every civilized country upon the globe! Among those who thus cast their all with Chicago was the subject of this brief address, and to no other individual is this city more indebted.

In the quaint old graveyard at Colchester, Conn., can be seen tombs of generations of the Wrights. Capt. Joseph Wright moved from Wethersfield to Colchester, where he purchased a large farm. He died Sept. 10, 1766, aged 87. His wife was Mary Dudley from Guilford. Timothy was their second son. He died in 1756, aged 44. His wife was Mehetible Brainard of E. Haddam. Their sixth child was John, born May 27, 1745. He died June 6, 1826. His wife was Lucy Sears of E. Haddam. Their fourth child was John, born Nov. 25, 1783. He died in Chicago, Ill., Sept. 20, 1840. He was born and raised on a large farm near Colchester, Conn., and having a store in Sheffield, Mass., he there, in 1814, married Huldah, a daughter, eldest but one, of Stephen Dewey. At the latter's house in Sheffield their eldest child, the subject of this sketch, was born July 16th, 1815. He was named John Stephen after both grandfathers.

In 1815-16, John Wright traveled for his health on horseback from Massachusetts into Illinois, and thence to New Orleans, whereby he acquired a knowledge of the country, and became much impressed with its promise for the future. He moved from Sheffield to Williamstown in 1822, where the mountain scenery is grandest of Berkshire, to have the benefits of the college in educating his children, having three sons at that time, John S., Timothy, and Walter. He continued a merchant. A brother of his wife, very dear to her, Prof. Chester Dewey, was in the college, and Mr. Wright at once took one of the best students, Mr. Willey from New Hampshire, into his family, giving him board for his teaching the children. The mother had been the teacher exclusively. She was a highly-cultivated lady in every respect, and taught her son, John S., before he was seven years of age, all the arithmetic, English grammar, and geography that he ever studied. Mr. Willey put him at Latin, which was his chief study for four years. Both parents were very superior in mental powers, perfectly united in family affairs, most devoted to their children! At ten, he was put with his brother, Timothy, with Mr. Bradley, going to his room in college to study and recite, and began Greek. After two or three years, an academy was started under a Mr. Canning, and to Latin and Greek, Algebra and Euclid were added. His excellent uncle, Prof. Chester Dewey, had such a fame for interesting scholars in study and arousing their ambition, that Mr. Pomeroy of Pittsfield, father of his then wife, built for him the Berkshire Gymnasium, and induced him to take charge of it as a higher field of usefulness. To him John S. was sent in 1829–30, and was then taken into his father's store as a clerk for six months, with an interest in part of the business, giving a trial of his book-keeping, which had been well mastered. The profits paid for another year's schooling at his excellent uncle's, who loved him as his own children, and never chided for anything, except that love of chess prevented adequate out-door exercise. Ambition was aroused equal to his uncle's pride and confidence, and the two and one-half years' discipline of head and heart was worth double all other education, except that of his adored parents! Yet the great and good Dr. Griffin, Professors Kellogg, Albert and Mark Hopkins, who succeeded Dr. G. in the presidency of the college, had ever a pleasant word of encouragement, bespeaking strong interest that helped abundantly his ambition to

make himself a man. I have heard that Prof. Hopkins
said, his was one of the brightest minds that ever
came under his instruction.

The first Sunday in June, 1832, he became a member of the Congregational Church. The wish so dear
to many a New-England mother was not absent from
his own, and she had always trained him to love the
ministry and study for that profession; but he pre-
ferred an active business life as giving far greater
opportunities for rising, and he expected to enter a
store at New York; but his uncle, Prof. Dewey, said
to him: "Cousin John, you will do no such thing;
your father intends to take you to the 'Far-West' and
let you make a man of yourself; and that's my own
advice as the best way to bring you out." The lad's
satisfaction was intense, and in a few weeks he went
home, expecting to go with his father to New York to
get a stock of merchandise. The cholera then first
appearing, the father thought it best not to take his
son; but the next day brought a letter from his
brother, Amasa, living in Brooklyn, saying the
cholera had subsided. The son started for the great
city, and found his way to his uncle's, to their great
surprise. But he told them he had no idea of going
way off West, without seeing New York; that he
hoped to help build a great city out there. Goods,
some $5000 or $6000 worth, were bought and shipped
to Buffalo, where from thence they had no idea. The
Black-Hawk War had that year called attention to
Chicago, where was Fort Dearborn; and a schooner
being found at Buffalo thither bound, the goods to

arrive were contracted for transportation. The plan was to get them to Galena, then prominent for its lead-mines. The trip from Williamstown, then consuming nearly three weeks, would be interesting to contrast with the present.

The father and son arrived at Chicago, October 29, 1832. In a few days the father purchased a horse to explore the land, going to Fox River and down it some thirty miles, and striking back for Chicago. He stopped a night at a place afterward called Plainfield, with a Mr. Searcy, who had a lot 80 x 150 feet, on north side of Lake Street, a little east of Clark, in Chicago. This Mr. Wright bought for $100. In 1833, he built a hewed-log store on this lot. It was called the "Prairie Store," being so far back from the line of business. Before the fire, it paid among the best rents in Chicago. The goods in part only arriving, some not reaching Buffalo when the vessel had to sail, John S. rented a store-room in a log-building of Mark Beaubien, with whom he boarded. Beaubien had met them on the South Branch, where they stood with the wagon, waiting to go over to another hotel. He was a large, fine-looking Frenchman, and came up, touching his hat and bowing, said, "You going to stop here?" Mr. Wright said, "Yes, we had heard the hotel was on the other side." Said Beaubien, with usual emphasis, raising and lowering his arm with a vengeance, "This my house. Me keep tavern like ——

('What I decline to repeat;
It was th name af a bad place, for mention unmeet';)

play de fiddle like damnation; you no stop with me?"

Mr. Wright was so amused that with a hearty laugh
he accepted the cordial invitation.

John S. had unpacked, marked, and was selling the
goods at 100 to 150 per cent advance, having learned
of Dole, Hogan, and Bob Kinzie, friends already, what
they charged. So when his father returned, he never
said a word about Galena, but told his son with much
glee of his lot purchase ; but the son "went him
better" by telling him that Philo Carpenter had proposed, just after he started to see the country, that
they should hold the chain for each other, and get
Mr. Herrington to survey for each a quarter-section,
to get at $1.25 per acre by pre-emption. The father
had a severe contest with Hiram Pearson to get his
quarter-section, but succeeded, although under the
adverse claim it was sold at $1000 per acre in 1836.
It is now Wright's Addition to Chicago, and includes
Union Park, and is worth millions. The son became
very expert with the rifle, and shot prairie-chickens
and snow-birds from the store-door, at the southeast
corner of Lake and Market Streets. The father
returned to Massachusetts in the fall, but came sud-
denly upon the son in the spring, and opened his eyes
with astonishment when he saw the store converted
into a gunnery, and the goods all sold. He said
naught to the son, but inquired of Mr. Dole about
him, who said, "Never you fear for John. The boys
(Hogan, Kercheval, Bob Kinzie, and Brady) have
tried their best to get him into our frolics, but he was
no go." He had spent the time studying the Greek
classics, etc. He assisted in raising the third frame-

building in Chicago in February or March, 1833—
P. F. W. Peck's store.

In 1834, Mr. John Wright removed his family to
Chicago. In 1833, the Rev. Jeremiah Porter organ-
ized the first Presbyterian church of all the Northwest, except at Galena. Mr. Wright was one of the
elders, and his son John S. an original member.

John Wright lived until Sept. 20, 1840, and day by
day had his original convictions strengthened that this
was to be the site of a populous city. His wife died
in Chicago, April 15, 1853, leaving an enviable record
of good works. She was one of seven sisters, and
the words of another may be applied to her:

"Distinguished no less for grace and loveliness of person
than for rare endowments of mind and heart, she grew up in
her New-England home in an atmosphere of the purest chris-
tian love and refinement; and giving up home and kindred,
she went forth trustfully to share with her husband in all
sweetness of patience and tenderness of devotion the hard-
ships and trials of life in the log-dwelling at Chicago."

The family home was for many years at the south-
west corner of Michigan Avenue and Madison Street.
She entered actively into every good work, and her
charity never failed. From her John S. Wright in-
herited most noble traits.

The lad, John S., became at once imbued with a
deep faith in the future of Chicago, and began to
operate in real estate on his own account in 1834.
He was not of age, but gave his father a lot valued at
$2000, in December, 1835, for the remaining seven
months of his minority. This was afterward returned

to him in the division of his father's estate. He published one of the first lithographic maps of this city early in 1834. It comprised Sections 9 and 16, and the fractional 10 and 15, bounded north by Chicago Avenue, south by Twelfth Street, west by Halsted Street, east by Lake Michigan. But only 10; the south half of 9, east of Jefferson Street; and the two or three north tiers of blocks of 16 were subdivided into lots; all the rest was in squares and 40 x 80 acre lots. In 1836, the property he had acquired was valued at $300,000, and this he had accumulated without pecuniary assistance from his father. He purchased at one time over 7000 acres of canal lands, and probably owned a greater portion of Chicago than any other person. As stated, he was a member of the first Presbyterian church. He also assisted in organizing a Sunday-school, in which he taught a class, and was likewise secretary and librarian, carrying this the first Chicago Sunday-school library, of 20 volumes, to and fro in his pocket-handkerchief.

In 1836, in accordance with his father's wishes, he purchased a warehouse and dock lots for $23,000, to engage in the shipping business, as the father considered it very desirable for the son of twenty-one to have regular occupation to promote good habits. His entire indebtedness at this time was about $25,000, and there was due him nearly $20,000, chiefly final payments upon real estate which he had sold; but the panic of 1837 brought ruin to many; his debtors could not pay, and by 1840, his property had all gone.

In 1837, he erected the *first* public-schoolhouse of

this city at his own expense ($507.93). It was on the church lot S.-W. cor. Clark and Washington sts. His mother was interested in an infant-school, and desiring a building, this dutiful and generous son erected it. This was the beginning of our public-school system, and for years he devoted much time and thought to educational matters. In 1839, he was manager of the Chicago Colonization Society, as well as trustee, secretary, and manager of the Union Agricultural Society. The farming interests engaged much of his attention, so that, in the fall of 1840, he began issuing *The Prairie Farmer*, hoping by practical agriculture to reach the leading farmers, the power of the West, upon the fundamental subject, common-school education! For some years he was sole editor, and retained an interest until the panic of 1857. Did time permit, I would fain dwell upon the value of this paper to all the Northwest.

From 1840–5, he traveled in a buggy most of the time in all parts of the then West—Indiana, Illinois, Wisconsin, and Iowa—to become acquainted with influential farmers, and to make them write for their paper, and advocate common schools. He became well informed about the country, and witnessed its rapid settlement, as well as the development of its unequalled, inexhaustible resources. In 1842, he got up the first State convention at Peoria, to promote an interest in common schools. It was a grand success, and he was made chairman of the committee to memorialize the legislature. Traveling then constantly to and fro about *The Prairie Farmer*, he had done noth-

ing toward the memorial when he went to Springfield,
but it was done, as he said, "after a fashion," and read
by him in the senate-chamber to the joint committees
of the senate and house upon common schools. Mon-
day morning the memorial was offered in the senate,
and Mr. Constable, from a Wabash county, and an
entire stranger to him, arose upon the presentation,
and said he had listened to its reading before the committees, and he moved to print 10,000 copies that it
was the best thing he ever saw or heard upon that
subject. Not a voice did he hear against it, but so
afraid was the lieutenant-governor (John Moore) of
Yankee-school innovations that he pettishly declared
the motion lost. Then 5000 was moved, and it
passed unanimously. That started the efforts in the
whole West for that great work.

In 1845-6, he was in the East, and wrote a series
of most valuable papers, appearing in *The Commercial
Advertiser, Evening Post, American Railroad Journal*, etc., etc., urging the capitalists of the East to
engage in the construction of railroads ; about the
various agricultural products of the West, their profits,
etc. ; the minerals, manufacturing advantages, the
canal, etc., etc., and predicting that Illinois bonds,
then worth 25 to 30 cents on the dollar, and three
years of accrued interest not reckoned, so prevalent
was the impression that the State debt could never be
paid; that by 1858-9, Illinois *would* pay her full interest without any increase in the then rate of taxation. Writing in 1860, he said: "And for two years
we *have* done this, and our bonds are above par!"

Who can measure the value of these writings and the good they accomplished, not only for Chicago, but for the Northwest?

On Sept. 1, 1846, he married, at the residence of Mrs. Jane C. Washington of Mt. Vernon, a niece of hers, Miss Catherine B. Turner, the youngest child of Henry S. Turner of Jefferson County, Virginia. She was handsome, witty, and accomplished, and her childhood, passed chiefly at Mt. Vernon after her mother's death, had been such as comes to few of us. Abandoning all the delights of Washington society, leaving her devoted friends and kindred, she came to the embryo city with her husband, as his mother had done before her, and for over a third of a century it has been her home. His marriage stirred ambition again to make money on Chicago property, and he bought most judiciously. In fact, in 1856, the ground-rent on two of the lots purchased for $13,500 was $7000 per annum, and his real estate was then valued at over $600,000, a great fortune in those days.

In 1847, he wrote a series of most valuable letters to the *Boston Courier*. These letters were commenced to urge upon the Bostonians the importance and advantage to themselves of subscribing liberally to the stock of the Galena-and-Chicago Union Railroad. In 1848, another series were published simultaneously in *The Boston Mining Journal and Railroad Gazette*, advocating the construction of railroads and presenting the advantages. His acquaintance was very large, and when the canal convention met in Chicago in 1847, he could name each State's representatives in the procession as it passed by, personal acquaintances. Among his many friends were the Kennicotts. The "Old Doctor," as he was familiarly known, became the horticultural editor of *The Prairie Farmer*, while Hiram wrote frequently also for the paper. Few among my older hearers have not enjoyed the hospitality of their delightful homes, and the friendship formed early in the forties, has now extended to the third generation!

In 1847, he proposed an extended system of parks for the three divisions of this city to be connected by boulevards. After the lapse of many years, this has been carried out, but at greatly-increased cost. Chicago owes not a little to his efforts in behalf of her park system. In 1848, he predicted that Chicago would increase in population twenty per cent per annum for five years, eighteen per cent per annum for the next five years. These were realized; but sixteen per cent for the next, and fourteen per cent for the succeeding five years, were not realized, and he considered the war an abundant reason. He calculated twelve per cent for the next five years, and then ten per cent indefinitely. His prediction in 1861, that our population in 1886 would be one million, has not been realized. The United-States census shows the rate of increase for the entire country has diminished, and the many flourishing suburban towns, Pullman, South-Chicago, etc., etc., have absorbed what would otherwise have been an addition to this city's population, and were it not for them, he would not have been far wrong. Many of you will remember the ridicule his predictions excited. He was far in advance of his age!

One who was afterward among the millionaires of Chicago objected to his efforts in behalf of the Galena-and-Chicago Union Railroad, arguing against it "because railroads would stop the advent of the 'prairie schooners,' 500 to 1500 teams then daily arriving; and with their stoppage, grass would grow in the street," was his sagacious declaration. Another objected to his efforts in behalf of the Illinois-Central Railroad. Said he, "Why, don't you see that the railroad will enable farmers to run off their produce to Cairo while the canal and river are frozen, which, if kept till spring, would have to come to Chicago." In 1847, before Chicago possessed a single railroad, he predicted a number of lines that would be built, afterward among our chief roads; and in 1858, he could say exultingly, "Wild as were these views considered, instead of the five railroads anticipated, we have *twelve* important trunk lines"; and surely he did his part to effect this result.

The Hon. William B. Ogden's memory needs no word of mine. Your archives contain his life. Yet with all his ability, even he did not see the future in store for this city as did John S. Wright. Mr. Ogden said in his first annual report as president of the Galena-and-Chicago Union Railroad, "It can not have escaped the observation of all acquainted with the region of country to be affected by the construction of this important work, that if constructed now and extended east from Chicago, around the head of

Lake Michigan, till it meets the Michigan-Central, as it soon will be, it secures to the country through which it passes, *the great Northwestern thoroughfare for all time to come*. No other continuous route of railroad will ever be made to that great and rapidly-improving country lying west and northwest of Lake Michigan to the north of the southern end of that lake, if this road is established there first. No line to the south of it, near enough to compete with it, will be at all likely to be built while the business of the country can be prosecuted upon the road on which we are now engaged," etc. In after-years he admitted to Mr. Wright his better insight into the future; and in 1868, the latter said, "Hon. W. B. Ogden is now the acknowledged railway king of the West; and although he used to consider my calculations extravagant, no other man living, so far as I know, has so anticipated the importance of railways to this city, present and prospective."

In 1848, Mr. Wright worked hard for a land-grant to secure a north-and-south railroad for Illinois. He wrote, printed, and distributed at his own expense, 6000 copies of petitions to congress in aid of a railroad from the upper and lower Mississippi to Chicago. Three different ones were prepared for the South, Illinois, and the East. His friend Stephen A. Douglas said they came to Washington by the hundred, numerously signed, and had much influence, being the earliest movement for this object outside of congress, except the Cairo Company. He went personally to Washington, and spent weeks in laboring for the passage of this bill. Sept. 20, 1850, it became a law. Congress thereby established a precedent of granting lands in aid of railroad construction. In the 41st congress, bills were pending to grant 189,-224,920 acres of the public land to railroads; and *The New-York Herald* estimated that previous congresses had granted 220,000,000 acres. This first land-grant was for 2,595,053 acres, to be taken by odd numbers in alternate sections within six miles of the railroad. Poor estimated the cost of the road at $30,000,000, and the value of the land at an equal amount.

John S. Wright published a pamphlet in which he insisted "that the State would be everlastingly dishonored if the legislature did not devise laws to build the road, and disenthrall the State of its enormous debt besides, out of the avails of this land-grant." I believe he was in favor of the State's constructing the road. Had this been done under equally honest and able management, it might have changed our entire railroad system. The land-grant would have paid for the road, and the State could have either derived the profit that has gone to the stockholders in dividends, and the stock is today quoted at 1.29½, or have given its citizens the benefits in lower rates and fares. It could have regulated the profits of other roads, as they are now regulated by water transportation, and the granger movement and outcry against railroad monopolies would never have existed. The legislature decided to transfer the land-grant to a corporation. Mr. Wright then insisted that in return therefore the said corporation should, during the continuance of its existence, pay *ten per cent* of its gross earnings from operation to the State in lieu of other taxes. The legislature in its wisdom reduced this payment to seven per cent, although after the bill had passed, the president of the Illinois-Central Railroad told him they *would* have paid the ten per cent rather than relinquish the project. These payments had amounted to $9,833,258.61, Oct. 31, 1884, and paid the State debt. So far as I know, no other State possesses a like revenue, and Illinois owes these millions chiefly to the efforts of John S. Wright.

In 1851, to make more money for himself, and at the same time benefit the farmers who suffered from a scarcity of hands, he engaged in the manufacture of the Atkins Self-Raking Reaper. Of this he said:

"Mr. Atkins, a bedridden mechanic, invented the Automaton Self-Raking Reaper, and gave me a half-interest to patent and introduce it. He had the perfection of ingenuity and mathematical skill to calculate the dimensions of each piece to bring about the required motion for raking, an entirely new automatic movement in mechanics, though he had never seen a reaper at work; and from his drawings made a model. The first reaper was made from that model, twelve times enlarged and never altered; yet its first trial was perfect in the harvest-field. I built one in 1852; 40 in '53; 300 in '54; 1200 in '55; and 2800 in '56, and never enough to supply the demand. The cost of the machine was $90, and it sold for $180 cash, credit, $200. Though the business seemed very promising, a providential circumstance caused its failure. In the winter of '54 and '55, I contracted for ash lumber to build 3000 machines for 1856. It was stuck up to season on the docks at several lake ports; but the summer of 1855, there was so much railroad iron coming here, and so little grain to

2

go down, that freight prices were inverted. I waited therefore for fall freights to reduce prices up the lakes. I contracted for four cargoes in October; but the vessels took
other freight at higher rates, and I made another contract;
but winter set in four weeks earlier than ever before known,
and two cargoes were frozen up in the St. Clair River, whence
it could not be got. It was the thickest lumber for the frames
and the most essential to have well seasoned. As a conse-
quence, contracts were made with mills all about here.
Superheated steam kiln-dryers were erected, and a contract
let to parties at Dayton, Ohio, to build 1000 machines, each
to be tested in the shop, and then delivered in Baltimore.
Having myself to choose whether to supervise here or at
Baltimore, I left for Baltimore. Two thousand machines
were built here of green lumber, and as each one was fully
warranted, and they went to pieces under the burning harvest
sun, an outlay of about $200,000 was required to make good
this loss. The Dayton machines were not tested, and proved
to be defectively constructed."

The crops were poor in '57. A panic swept over
the country. His debtors could not pay, and with the
utter prostration of real estate, his property was swept
entirely away. I have dwelt at length upon this
matter to show you that this failure was caused by a
combination of circumstances that no human eye could
have forseen. The panic of 1857 brought ruin to
many thousands besides himself!

In 1859, he formed a project for a land company,
which in its magnitude was worthy of his gigantic in-
tellect. His excellent legal friend, the late H. M.
Morfit of Baltimore, was his counsel. In 1860, he
published a pamphlet in aid of this land-improvement
company. He obtained an option on thousands of

acres, two million dollars worth, extending in a belt entirely around this city in 1867, at from $65 to $450 per acre. In 1871, it was worth in some instances $20,000 per acre. In 1861, a charter was obtained from the Illinois legislature, and he went to New York to arrange with a good friend, Mr. James T. Soutter, ex-president of the Bank of the Republic, who had unbounded influence upon capitalists; but ill-health and other reasons sent him to Europe, and while awaiting his return, Mr. Wright began the study of international law, to which he devoted seven years. Charles O'Connor examined some of the manuscript containing articles for *The Journal of Commerce,* and, upon finishing, he remarked: "Mr. Wright, you are surely right as to your views of the nature of our institutions." This work grew day by day, until it resulted in a volume, entitled, "State Sovereignty— National Union." Mr. O'Connor was seen by him repeatedly, from time to time, as the work progressed. By the spring of 1863, he had gone carefully through Barbyrae's French Pufendorf and Grotius, annotating on loose sheets. Prof. S. B. F. Morse had been his intimate friend for years, and introduced him to his brother, Finley, who was engaged in the same line of study. Finding the translations of classic works worse than nothing, and himself so rusty in the language so well known in childhood, he went to Prof. Morse and told him he must have the assistance of a thorough Greek and Latin scholar. He sent him to his friend, Prof. J. Holmes Agnew, who at once engaged with his whole heart and soul in helping. This

volume met with a cool reception from the public; but
President Hopkins wrote: "It is the most wonderful
gathering of the great ideas of the world upon the
depths of politics; but my chief wonder is how a man
always so devoted to business could possibly have got
the scarce old books to get the writings, that the evi-
dence of our errors and the uniform tracing of them
to their sources is the strangest event in our history."
In January, 1862, he wrote to the *Evening Post* on
the federal debt, from which I extract:

"We must pay whatever rate is necessary to get the
money—the sinews of war. But with the reëstablishment of
the Union will return a new and firmer confidence in the
perpetuity of our institutions, and a still stronger and more
rapid career of prosperity than we have ever known, and the
value of government securities will have a corresponding
advance in value. There is no propriety or necessity, it
appears to me, in allowing the bulk of this advance to enure
to the speculators, either home or foreign, who will be the
owners of most of this indebtedness, and who will in the
main not have advanced the money now when it is needed,
but will have bought it up just as soon as they see the ordeal
is passed, and our institutions are to be permanent. Government sixes are now under ninety. They have heretofore
sold at one hundred and twenty-four, or higher, and with a
return of confidence will go there again, and even beyond.
We wish no stain of repudiation to rest upon our untarnished
federal credit, such as rests upon the British government for
striking down its rate of interest; and yet there is no propriety in our paying more than other nations whose securities are not half what are ours. I would therefore propose
that a stipulation should be inserted in each loan-bill, and
alluded to in the bonds; that as the stock advances *above*

par, for each five per cent of increase the rate of interest shall be reduced, say a half of one per cent; perhaps also giving the holder the option of demanding payment of the principal, though this option appears to me unnecessary and inexpedient. * * * With financial skill, the government can advance its credit so that in a few years, if this proposition be practicable, the interest will be reduced one-third or one-half."

Has not the result demonstrated the wisdom and value of these ideas? Government bonds bearing three per cent interest are now above par!

In the excitement of the war he thought his land company would have no chance, and it was not resumed until after the fall of Richmond. In 1867, he began to prepare a pamphlet urging upon capitalists the many advantages of investing in Chicago property; but the work grew until it resulted in a volume entitled, "Chicago—Past, Present, and Future." His mind was now so disordered that the book contained much irrelevant to the subject, but eschewing that it was a work of incalculable value to this city, and the labor he gave to it was very great. The press spoke of it in the most flattering words, but it had a very limited sale. He was in Chicago at the time of the great fire, and his vivid description was as follows:

"I was sleeping in a room adjoining my office on East-Washington Street that memorable Sunday night. About two o'clock a.m., a man came thumping at my door, and supposing it a drunken loafer who was trying to find his room, I made no reply. After three or four tremendous thumpings, he cried out, very loud, 'Mr. Wright, are you in here?' and I asked crossly, 'What do you want?' Said he, 'Mr. Wright, the whole city is on fire, and this building will be burnt in a few minutes.' I turned over to the window, and sure enough, the large and blazing coals made me close it; and I put on my clothes quicker than ever before, by the light of the fire, and went on the first floor. Dr. Heydock was there, things all moving. 'Why, Doctor,' said I, 'have we got to move?' He replied, 'This building will be burnt in a very few minutes.' I returned to my room and did up, in some large paper, a Geneva Bible and a lot of business papers, including deeds, which I had put together most providentially. With these and a satchel, all I could carry, I went out to see the extent of the fire, with gratitude unspeakable to my God and the kind janitor, for my wonderful escape. I started to join my daughter, who was ill at my old friend, Dr. George E. Shipman's, on North-Peoria Street. I tried to cross the South Branch at VanBuren Street, but at Adams Street, on State, I saw it was impossible, and went north to cross the river at State Street; but, in this short space of time, the flames had reached the stable on the river. The large coals were falling so thickly over the North Division, as well as the South, that I could not save my papers going through the terrible rain of fire. At Lake Street, I turned again for Twelfth Street, and oh! the grandeur of that immense sheet of flame as it rose about three o'clock from the very centre of our city! Thence crossing the river at Twelfth Street, I soon came to the buildings where the fire started, and left my papers with a housekeeper on the edge. I then had a walk of a mile and a-third in the rear and beside the flame; so that no one could have more realized the unexampled conflagration. About four o'clock, my daughter's intense anxiety was relieved! With what power and gratitude my head and heart then worked upon the future of our city! I saw in this calamity sure benefits!

"The next morning, upon getting my things to go to the Adams House, never dreaming that the fire had crossed State Street, I was hailed by D. H. Horton, one of the publishers of my Chicago book, who was sitting upon a dray at the corner of Wabash Avenue and Congress Street. He informed me of the destruction of the North as of the South Side, and his salutation was, 'Well, Wright, what do you think *now* of the future of Chicago?' I thought an instant and replied, 'I will tell you what it is, Horton. Chicago will have more men, more money, more business, within five years than she would have had without this fire.' Though the remark was well spread at once, few realized the truth."

Not long after this that noble mind gave way so completely that Mr. Wright had to be placed in an insane asylum. He died in the Pennsylvania Hospital for the Insane, Sept. 26, 1874, and was interred at Rose Hill, Sept. 29. The friends of many years who acted as pall-bearers were: Philo Carpenter, Gurdon S. Hubbard, E. S. Wadsworth, B. W. Raymond, Hiram Kennicott, S. Lind, W. Osborn, William Bross, T. B. Carter, and George R. Clarke. His life's work was done, and his great spirit returned to God, who gave it!

> "Like shadows gliding o'er the plains,
> Or clouds that roll successive on,
> Man's busy generations pass;
> And while we gaze, their forms are gone.

> "He lived, he died—behold the sum,
> The abstract of the historian's page—
> Alike in God's all-seeing eye,
> The infant's day, the patriarch's age.

> "To crowd the narrow space of life
> With wise designs and virtue's deeds,
> So shall we wake from death's dread night
> To share the glory that succeeds."

As stated by Crocker:

"Dryden's aphorism, that great wit, meaning mental powers generally, is nearly allied to insanity, is so true as to have become a proverb; but it stands on older and graver authority, that of Seneca."

I trust enough has been said to convince you of his wonderful mental powers, which for so many years he used for the good of this city, that he loved so well. Judge Jameson wrote:

"As the magnetic currents are said to play about the earth, enveloping it in a net-work of living forces, so thought plays about every subject of human interest. Thinking minds try to trace out causes and to forecast results."

This John S. Wright did! Speaking of life, he said:

"Laboring as we do almost exclusively for self and for this life, as practical and wise men, we should ever remember that as to time the individual is of no account, a miserable, despicable creature, except, precisely, as he fulfills his obligations to his city, to his State, to the nation, to his fellow-men, to his God! Man has not wisdom to do himself any good whatever, except as he seeks to promote the good of his own family, of his own church, of his own State, of his own nation. He may live and consume for his own good his *quantum* of food, drink, and clothing; but *cui bono ?* "

I believe that the time will come when Chicago must appreciate the magnitude and benefit of his life's work. Few of her citizens today realize all that he did in the past. Andreas' "History of Chicago" contains the following:

"The extracts here given might, in the absence of other information, lead to a misconception concering the character of John S. Wright. Although a born trader and a bold speculator, he was a man of rare virtues, and during his long residence in Chicago, was identified with nearly every enterprise and measure calculated to promote its prosperity or elevate the educational, mental, moral, or religious standards of the city. The benefactions of this wonderfully energetic citizen permeated nearly every channel of the life and shewed in every phase of her early growth. The building of the early railroads, the development of manufactures, the first Presbyterian church, Sabbath-schools, and the common-school system of the State, the Press; to all these he devoted his energies and gave in no stinted measure. Frequent mention of him appears elsewhere in this volume."

Upon hearing of his death, Gen. John A. Clarke wrote to me:

"Your father was one of my earliest Illinois friends. About the same age, we spent the winter of 1833–4 in Chicago together; boarded at the same log-cabin (Rufus Brown's), slept in the same bunk under the counter in your grandfather's store, on the corner of Water and State Streets, and during all the years that followed, until your father was stricken with the disease that terminated his life here, our friendship was unbroken. This friendship and the incidents of our early association are remembered with a lively interest. I shall always think of him as he was in his days of usefulness, when all things were possible to him; when to suggest the failure of his great plans was to almost excite him to anger, so certain was he of the future."

J. Wingate Thornton of Boston wrote to me:

"I am glad to hear from you, and the account of your father's last days are painfully interesting. He was a far-sighted, sagacious man, much above the average, and had he found fellows of equal intelligence and rectitude, the story had been far happier! I envy not the callous indifference and stupidity which failed to sustain the plans which capital in intelligent hands would have carried to public and private good. * * * In the future it will be found that Chicago will hold in honorable remembrance the name of John S. Wright as one of the best men; a pioneer in the cause of common schools, popular education, and as one who distinctly pointed out the elements which would make her the great central mart of the United States. Time will vindicate his name and fame."

The Rev. J. Ambrose Wight wrote to me when I informed him of this my proposed paper:

"I am glad to recall to the public mind the service your father did, not for Chicago alone, but for Illinois, and in fact for the then Northwest. I came to Chicago to live and to be in his employ in May, 1843, and was with him on salary or as partner till the close of 1855, with a short exception. He had a clearer insight of what Chicago was to be than any other man I knew in that time. His mind, like that of his mother, ran upon public interests; not those specially of the nation, but of his own city, State, and neighborhood. He was constantly planning in the earlier part of this time for these interests. He saw clearly that Illinois was to be a great State, and Chicago a great city. His habit of forecast in these matters often brought upon him ridicule from those who were content with things, as they were, and resisted improvements. As his modes of expressing his convictions and impulses, I recall his establishment of *The Prairie Farmer*. There was not another man in the State at that time who would have done it. And few had, at first, faith in his success with it. And though he had no special training for such an undertaking, not being bred a farmer, he carried it on successfully for two years, and established it. The event shewed his prescience. There was need of just such a paper at that time. The settlers upon prairie lands had no guide in regard to a great number of questions which it was necessary to settle, and only experience and intercommunication could settle them: 'Will the cultivated grasses grow on these prairie lands?' 'Can sheep be successfully kept here?' Will our accustomed fruits succeed? and what kind shall we cultivate, and how treat them?' 'How shall we fence these open lands?' These and the like questions, now of far less difficulty, if any, were then matters of great moment; for the settlers were poor and could not afford experiments. The matter of harvesting crops, too, was one in which the paper was an active and influential instrument.

"There was another great interest which nobody attended to till Mr. Wright led off in it. I mean that of public-school education. Illinois had no *system* of schools. Such as were in existence were private or local affairs. He worked up a system of public schools, and, I think, drafted a law, which he talked and wrote into favor, and got it through the legislature, which was then no easy matter, for the south part of the State was reluctant; but he had made the acquaintance of leading men all through the State, in all its neighborhoods; and that law is the basis of the school system of Illinois to this day. It has, of course, undergone many alterations. The school system of Chicago owes more to him for its inception than to any one man. It *started* by his efforts. There rallied to it, early, a body of men, whose names are attached to the several schools of the city today, while none that I am aware of bears his name. And very possibly those men have, if alive, forgotten that he was the man whose enthusiasm excited first their own. The reason for this is patent to those who knew him well. His perceptive faculties were not always supported by reflective ones. He saw and devised and grew enthusiastic till he had got others to take hold, when his interest in a matter often declined, and he did not carry out his schemes. This peculiarity attached to his management of his private affairs. He ought to have been immensely

wealthy. He bought with great sagacity, but his after-man-
agement was not successful. He did not adhere to and make
a success of his own good planning. As a sample: After he
had installed me in *The Prairie Farmer*, he left for New York
and Washington to be absent three weeks; but I neither saw
or heard from him in eleven months; yet when he returned
he had purchased a property which in a very few years was
valued at two millions of dollars. This peculiarity made him
seem visionary to many, and has caused his real shrewdness
and benevolent forecast to be forgotten.

"Another of his public acts I well remember. The State,
by the influence of the southern part of it, had passed a law
restricting interest to six or seven per cent. The merchants
of that section suffered farmers' accounts to run for a long
time, charging interest at high rates, which gave rise to the
law. It worked very badly for the north of the State, and
especially for Chicago; for money could not be loaned at six
per cent, and money was greatly wanted. Mr. Wright drew
up a brief law allowing ten per cent on money loaned. He
printed the law, with a brief argument for it, on slips, which
he sent by thousands through the State, and the law was carried, to the immense relief of Chicago, and, in fact, of the
whole State.

"Previous to this he had advocated with all his might and
assisted to secure the 'two-mill tax,' which relieved the State
of an incubus of debt of sixteen millions, and which operated
for some years to hold it back from prosperity. The law was
stoutly opposed, by its immigrant population especially, who
had brought with them from Europe a hatred of taxation,
though many of them had very little property to be taxed.

"I remember these things very well, for I not only heard
him talk enthusiastically of them, but in my way assisted him
in getting them before the public. I have always believed
that Chicago and the State owed him more than they knew
or at least recognized. He was a perfectly self-reliant man,

and the independence of his opinions often avoked for the time a distrust of them, or even an opposition to them; and his later misfortunes served perhaps to cause forgetfulness of the real services he had rendered to the public."

And now, in conclusion, to those among you who extended to him your friendship to the end, unalienated by the infirmities of disease, or the pecuniary misfortunes that came to him, I would tender my most sincere and heartful thanks!

Mr. Chairman, permit me to present to the Chicago Historical Society his portrait, in behalf of my brother, Chester Dewey, and myself. It was painted by his friend, Mrs. St. John, formerly of Chicago, now of New York, and represents him as he appeared at the age of fifty-five.

L. of C.

TRIBUTE OF HON. WILLIAM BROSS.

AT the close of the address, Ex-Lieut. Gov. Wm.
Bross moved that a vote of thanks be tendered to Mr.
Wright for his discriminating and very excellent ad-
dress. It was seconded and unanimously adopted.

On offering the resolution, Gov. Bross said that he
was very glad that his son, waiving all delicacy, had
spoken so freely and so fairly of the character and the
life-work of his eminent father, John S. Wright. It
was his good fortune to have known him long and well.
Indeed, he was the first citizen of Chicago with whom
he became acquainted, and it were well if each one's
recollection could dwell on incidents equally pleasant.
On his way to this city, in the early morning of May
12th, 1848, between Kalamazoo and St. Joseph, there
to take the steamer Sam Ward—that was four years
before the railways from the East reached Chicago—he,
with other passengers, became very tired of being
tumbled about in the stage coach. At the change of
horses, about daylight, Mr. B., with several others,
started ahead on foot, and the result was a very refresh-
ing walk of two or three miles. Here the speaker fell
in company with a slim, wiry man, whom he at once
found to be a most intelligent and courteous companion.

Chicago's position with reference to the system of lake navigation, and also with reference to the vast and fertile prairies between the lakes and the Rocky Mountains, and the certainty that it would become the commercial capital of the upper Mississippi valley, were all detailed in graphic and enthusiastic language by Mr. Wright to the willing ears of his listener, eager to gain all the information he could get in regard to the position and the prospects of his new home in the West. More than thirty-five years study and travel by stagecoach and steamer, and by all the main railway lines between the lakes and the Rocky Mountains, the building and commercial statistics of the city, now rounding up into the enormous amount of more than a thousand millions of dollars annually, have simply filled out the outlines of the picture given him that May morning in the wild woods of Michigan by John S. Wright. Is it any wonder that he should cherish the memory of Mr. Wright as one of the best informed and most interesting men he ever met.

This was not all. With his usual courtesy to strangers, he called at the hotel on the Sabbath, and took Mr. B. to his own seat in the Second Presbyterian church, and in the course of a week or two introduced him to Mayor Woodworth and most of the leading business men of the city.

In 1849 Mr. B. said he was the partner of the Rev. Dr. J. A. Wight in the publication of the *Prairie Herald*, and Mr. Wight was also the editor of the *Prairie Farmer*. As the office of the two papers was in the same room, he then saw much of Mr. Wright.

He often spent hours talking of the interests of the
farmers, in all their varied relations, showing an inti-
mate and accurate acquaintance with whatever could
promote their prosperity and welfare. Agricultural
implements, the most profitable crops and how they
could be best and most economically produced, har-
vested and brought to market; our lake marine and its
relations to the prosperity of the city and the vast farm-
ing districts west of it; Chicago as a successful manufacturing centre, because food for operatives must
always be cheaper here than anywhere else upon the
continent; railway prospects; in fact, everything that
related to the political and commercial interests of the
city and the Northwest, were discussed with a breadth
of comprehension and accuracy of detail that seemed
almost an inspiration from some source far above the
grasp of human intelligence.

The memorial has given many of the leading facts
and enterprises in the life-work of Mr. Wright, and
were it proper and did time permit, he would, if possible, add intensity and more extended illustration to the
biographical sketch. Take only a single example.
Mr. Wright was one of the first to see the importance
and grasp the possibility of a railway from the lakes to
the Gulf of Mexico. The land-grant which had successfully completed the Illinois-and-Michigan Canal,
furnished the text for a similar grant for this great
national railway project. Mr. Wright's pen did much
to make it familiar to the people, and in the winter of
1849–50 a bill was introduced into Congress making a
grant of lands to the states through which it would run

3

for the construction of the road. There it lay for
weeks and months, attracting very little attention.
Mr. Wright saw what action was needed, and that he
was the man that must take it. At his own expense
he printed thousands of circulars, stating briefly the
necessity of the road to the welfare of the nation, with
a petition to Congress to pass the bill. At that time
such documents went by mail free to postmasters, and
to his personal knowledge he kept his clerk busy for
weeks sending these to every postmaster between the
lakes and the Gulf. The requests to the postmasters
to get signers and forward the petitions to their con-
gressmen were promptly attended to, and in the early
summer sessions of Congress the petitions came in by
thousands, and members were astonished at the unani-
mous demand of their constituents for the railway.
Thus our Senators Douglas and Shields and Representatives Wentworth and others saw their opportunity,
and the bill was passed Sept. 20, 1850. Now look at
our thousands of miles of railway, and grasp, if you
can, the influence they have upon the growth, the hap-
piness and the prosperity of this city and the great
Northwest. The money and the moving spirit that
started effectively this wonderful progress were furnished by John S. Wright.

In according the leading position thus given to Mr.
Wright in this and other improvements, it may be
asked what was left for the founders of the city—great
men they certainly were—to do ? He was the leading
spirit mainly in the intuitive perceptions he had of the
forces on which his predictions of the future greatness

of the city and of the country tributary to it were
founded. Like many others, his mind ran too far
ahead of his cotemporaries to be appreciated. He
lived a generation before his time. Hence he was
considered by many a dreamer—a man whose conclusions could not be trusted. While he was great and
grasping as to the events of the future, hundreds and
thousands of others, by their substantial character and
steady purposes, wrought directly to the fulfilment of
Mr. Wright's conclusions. They had and held the
position among the capitalists and leading business
men of the country that gave them the command of the
means to build warehouses, move our crops, transport
them over the great lakes; establish banks, build and
run our railways, and generally to secure the prosperity
and the progress of the Northwest. Such men were
Wm. B. Ogden, John B. Turner, B. W. Raymond,
Gurdon S. Hubbard, Thomas Richmond, Charles
Walker, William H. Brown, Geo. Smith, Daniel Brainard, F. C. Sherman, J. Y. Scammon, and I might mention scores of others, most of whom are passed away—
all great men, whose substantial business character en-
abled them to accomplish results, from the very enthusiasm of his character impossible to Mr. Wright. It
would be absurd to attribute to any one man more than
a moiety of the grand results—more wonderful than
any achievements of the past—which the Queen City
of the lakes and the country, whose commercial centre
she is, have made a simple but substantial reality. Mr.
Wright could see in prophetic vision, and his sterling
common sense grasped the means and the character of

the great men around him, by whose efforts his splendid conceptions would be realized. Great and impossible as they then appeared, all men now will concede that our thousands of miles of railway, making Chicago the central station between the Atlantic and Pacific oceans; our vast commerce, derived from millions of intelligent, prosperous freemen, who are subduing the fertile regions west of us; our lake marine, carrying more than twice the values of the entire foreign traffic of the nation; our city, with its great stores and busy mannfactures, its tremendous live-stock interests, and its immense grain shipments, and its ceaseless growth, sure to round up to a million people before the century closes; these facts and such as these, patent to the comprehension of all mankind, have more than fulfiled all Mr. Wright's brightest anticipations. Let Chicago always hold his name in vivid and honored remembraance.

www.ingramcontent.com/pod-product-compliance
Lightning Source LLC
Chambersburg PA
CBHW021446090426
42739CB00009B/1669